# Letters from your soul

## Readings to rekindle the quest for freedom, joy and love

VICTOR NOBLE

Letters from your soul:
*Readings to rekindle the quest for freedom, joy and love*
Copyright © 2013 by Victor Noble

ISBN-13: 978-0992382001
ISBN-10: 0992382009

Silent Note publications, Sydney, Australia

# Contents

# Editor's Preface

*Letters from your soul* is a collection of selected readings done by Victor Noble from 2011 to 2013. The readings came about as a response to various interactions he had in his talks and personal sessions with people from all walks of life.

As his best friend and partner during the time of his awakening and being close to him in the years following his transition, I feel fortunate to have watched the amazing transformation of human consciousness first hand. My discussions with him before, during and after his experience have taken me through a journey filled with joy, pain, amazement, love, faith and wonder. Through this book, I share some of his words, which have helped me, and so many others, in following their own dreams.

The purpose of each reading in the book is to act as a call for enquiry within oneself. There is no method, instruction or path suggested in any of the writings. Instead, they are filled with insights that ignite a thirst for self-transformation.

As Victor said in one of his talks – "What I sell is already with(in) you. So, don't look for answers; look for a movement within yourself as you hear these words. The only thing of value, which you will ever get out, is the deepening of your own quest and the strengthening of your hope for finding your own answers".

Since each short piece was written to be read, in front of a small audience, you may want to read them out slowly to a loved one, or, to a small group to start a discussion or a meditation session.

The readings were not done originally for print and the structure may not be as well defined as you may expect in a published work. But, I have opted to leave each reading as it is, because the beauty of the message lay in its raw simplicity. There is also an abundance in the usage of pauses, line breaks and commas, to pace the reading.

As a final note, Victor's use of the word 'god' refers to the core substance of the universe. We all have different names for that one thing; he just uses the word god for its simplicity and to evoke the feelings of gratitude towards existence. His references to religious figures are also accidental and dependent on who the audience was. He does not favor or reject any particular religion, path or method more than the other.

Bini Noble, 11th December 2013

# *One*

## GRATITUDE

*I* am like a tree...
   the words you hear, are the fruits...
god, is the earth, on which I stand...

There are people in my life, who allowed me to grow,
kept me alive and helped me expand... they are my sun,
water and the sky...

And, the world gave me the winds... that moved me...
shaped me...
but, could never uproot me, from my earth...

If you have ever thanked the tree, for any of the fruits...
tree has always passed the thankfulness to the sun, the
water, the sky and the winds...

And most importantly, like all electricity is earthed...
all thankfulness goes to the earth on which it stands...

To his design, all thankfulness belongs...

Praise the design, which ensures that wherever there is
a tree rooted in his soil, there will be sun, water, winds
and sky...

Fall in love with his design... and have faith...
if he has given feet, he will give reasons to dance too...
if he has given voice, he will give seasons to sing too...
and, if he has given wings he will give skies to fly too...

The tree doesn't need anything in return, for its fruits...
it just wants you to take care of the fruit... there is no
bigger gift for a tree, than to have one seed from one of
these fruits to find the right soil...

So all of you, who come as fruit pickers have a very special place in its heart...
you are the reason tree even looks at a future...
for you, there is a future... for the tree, there is none...

You are the one, who has given it reasons to make
fruits... you are the reason blood flows in the tree...
the tree doesn't say this often... but it knows this
forever...

From each ray of sun, and each drop of water, from each fist of sky, and each inch of earth... the tree has taken its life...

The fruits that it gives, are nothing, compared to what it has taken...

A tree lives and dies in gratitude!

*Two*

## ROSES ARE RED

I wish you would love me more...
 I wish you were more successful...
I wish you didn't have that habit...
I wish you were just a little different...

Am I asking for too much?
...

While you wished all that...
I too wished the same...
I too wished you were just a little different...
I too wished that, all my life...

I had heard stories of people who did so much for love...
they changed so much for love...

But today I wonder...

why couldn't I change you, or, why couldn't you change me...

Maybe I got the stories wrong...
maybe we were both asking for too much...

Maybe love needed to be first, and the changes we wanted second...

Why did it take me a lifetime to see that where there is love, miracles follow...
why did it take me a lifetime to see that I just needed to love...

Each day that I wished you were different is the day I lost...

A day which could have been spent learning about my inability to love...

Maybe love is what I needed to change us...

Love when applied unconditionally has this effect on ourselves and others...
...

Apply it to your soul a few times a day, and let love take care of the changes...

Just love someone for once, for what they are...

love someone, not because it will make your life com-
fortable, but just because it will fix your soul... the
other may change, or may not, but your soul will say
thank-you to you...

The other may be selfish, may chase petty dreams and
fool you... the other may never learn the lessons, if you
don't say...

But don't be disheartened, because the biggest lesson
of all is love...
and at least one person in the relationship will get that
lesson...
and if you are filled with love it may spill onto the other
someday...

The other may walk away today, if you don't hold tight...
but rest assured, the other will run away one day, if you do...

Love brings people together pulling with delicate threads...
delicate threads of feeling connected with each other's
pain and joy...

Take care of the threads, which connect the heart...
don't try to replace the threads with ropes...
ropes are to pull rocks, but to pull a soul, you need these
threads...

Good or bad of the other is not the question, the question is whether you have the capacity to love...

Who you have is not the question, the question is whether you can love who is there with you...

What you get from the other is not the question, the question is can you love when you get nothing in return...

Love someone not for what they do for you...
but, because they give you a chance, to practice love...

Want someone not for what they give you...
but, because they give you a chance to give...

There is no value in the other person if you seek value...
there is value in the other, only because they evoke value in you...

All values, which you see outside of you, are your own projections and wishes...
the real value of the presence of the other, is in you...

Your net worth is not a loving husband or wife...
your worth is proportional to your capacity to love...

There is no need for the other to change...
by being what they are, they add value in your life...

Like a rose looks more beautiful with the stem...
a person, too, is more lovable with his/her leaves and thorns...

When did you stop seeing the other as a flower... and why did you...?

Roses are red... let them be so!

# Three

## FEAR

*What are you worried about?*
*What makes you so scared?*
*What has made you the slave of your insecurities?*

*Don't you see the cycle?*
*Imaginary fears, cause you to anticipate danger... in anticipation you prepare to defend... and in defence, you attack others... even before they have done anything to hurt you...*

*And, they do the same to you...*
*don't you see that the central point of your relation to the world is fear?*
*in fear you seek to relate... and in relating you seek security...*
*but when you begin from fear, you end in fear, in all your relationships...*

Who are you?

He introduced himself as somebody, and said he just saw me worried and thought that talking might help...

I didn't know what to say... it was none of his business... he did seem a bit crazy and weird... but at that point I felt like talking...

*You know how it is with these things...*
*you know your fears are valid and real, but you can't really tell when and where they live...*

*It was not so long ago when I was a child...*
*and I told the man, whose finger I was holding, that I am scared...*
*what are you afraid of? the man asked...*

*I am scared that I may lose you in this crowd...*
*I may never find you... someone might hurt me... or, someone might take me away...*

*The man said, don't leave my finger if you can...*
*you will never be lost, and you will never have anything to fear...*
*but if you do lose me, just remember what I say today...*
*we will find each other because both of us will be looking for each other...*
*it is not so difficult to find me... just try and remember the steps you took, after you lost me... and walk back...*

Not sure why, but I didn't feel scared after that for a long time...

Then I was a teenager, and I was sitting alone one day...
I was afraid that no one would ever look at me...
I was scared that nobody would ever like me...
I was afraid that people would never understand me...

There was nothing special about my fears...
I was just afraid that I would never be special...
I was just afraid like anyone else I guess...

But there was so much of life that lay ahead of me...
I never allowed those fears to take over my life...
I slowly learned to not entertain those thoughts...
I slowly learned to pretend and hide behind my looks and tricks...

Once in a while, my fears would come up when someone told me that I am not good enough...
not good enough for what? I was not sure though...
but these words used to scare me...

Life moved on...
I became better at not looking afraid... not being scared of anything... not being weak and not being vulnerable...

Now I am an adult... and you see... now I am not scared...
no really, I am not scared at all...

*Not sure why you had to repeat that...* he said with a smile.

I continued, before he could say anything more.

*I am not scared, but I am just worried sometimes, and my worries are all for real reasons...*

I said it again, but maybe he didn't notice.

*Isn't it your fear which now hides as worry?* he said...
*have you found a new name for being afraid, since being afraid is so uncool and being worried is so cool? The way your soul shivers when your job is in danger, or your partner looks at someone else, it shows that it is just your mortal fears which you talk about as concerns and worries...*

I didn't like that comment at all... what is his problem I thought... I ignored it, as I was wearing a better suit than him... I continued...

*Ok, may be it is just another name for fear, but let's not play with words here... let's just say I am afraid of certain things in life...*

*For example, I am afraid that my partner will walk away... and that keeps me constantly on guard... and because the best defence I've got is attack, I hurt my partner...*

*I am also afraid that I won't have enough money when I am old... so I stay fearful of my boss... I am afraid of anything that reduces my bank balance...*
*which ensures I live like a slave...*

*I have to do what I am supposed to do, otherwise I will be destroyed... I will be nobody...*

*That is my biggest fear, being a nobody... because all my life I thought I was somebody... all my life I was told I was somebody...*

*So you see my fears are all real and valid...*

*Sure they are real to you...* he said

I continued.

*I fear that someday it will all just end...*
*before I even notice...*
*strange emptiness fills my being, when I think of it...*

*It is just too troublesome to analyse all this...*
*I prefer to just not think about all this...*
*these thoughts make me more scared...*

*I try to avoid them, I don't have time for these thoughts, and I have a mortgage to pay...*

*Oh! That reminds me, I have to be somewhere,*

*I think I should leave now... not sure talking to you will help anyways...*
*you seem like one of those crazy spiritual kind, who have no clue at all, how things are in this world...*

*I mean you guys talk about love, death, god, universe etc etc... I am not sure if real fears can be addressed by talking about that stuff...*
*pure entertainment it is, for those who have less to worry about...*

*Ok, let's talk real then,* He said...
*let's just talk about the tunnel, and the darkness in the tunnel... let's see this darkness, before we talk about the light at the end of the tunnel...*

*How does one solve these fears?*
*do you think that tools which are born of fear, will help you solve your fear?*
*don't your protections have their root in fear, and do you think what is born of fear, will set you free from fear?*

*What do you mean?* I asked.

*I am saying that out of fear you prepare to defend, and you expect those defences to reduce fear...*
*all your defences have their roots in fear...*
*may it be your insurance schemes, or guns and contracts...*
*these solutions are all part of one big family, and they promote each other via fear...*

*Fear causes more insurances and more insurances cause more fear... you are scared that you won't have enough money later so you start paying someone money every month... that actually reduces your money... and, most importantly you become less capable... because now you are "covered", and by becoming less capable you become even more scared...*

*Similarly when you are scared of guns you buy one your-selves, and more guns just mean more fear in the world...*

*And your fear that your partner will love someone else more someday... makes you forever control and scare him/her... or you find someone else before he/she does... your relationships are full of fear because you sought them out of fear in the first place... you were scared to be lonely, so you made sure you find someone...*

*No wonder you are scared of so many things... because fear is the centre from which you are relating to the whole world...*
*...*

*I can see your point... I said*
*but, it is disturbing to hear all this, and moreover it is not solving any of my problems...*

*The fact is that the only defence I have is to fight and be covered... and I don't care if it is born of fear...*

*I just can't give up my defences, can I? How am I sup-posed to jump out of this vicious cycle? I didn't start it...*

*I am sure you can see better...* he said...

*May be we can look at it differently... let's answer a basic question to begin with, "what are you defending"?*

*I have lots to defend you know... I am defending my opinions when I argue... I am defending my future when I am scared of my boss... I am defending my habits when I fight... I am defending my beliefs when I refuse to hear... I am defending my image... and I am defending my identity...*

He smiled... and said, *I thought you will come up with a list of real things...*
*maybe you just look smarter than you are...*

I was furious... I felt like defending myself right then... I raised my voice.
*Don't you, in your dumbness, see that I am defending myself... and at least I am real...*

*Should I hit you on the head so that you know I am real...? don't you see it is important for me to defend myself...? don't you see that there are things I need to be worried about...? don't you see how important all this is to me...? don't you see I am real, and that I am important...?*

*Sorry! My bad!!* he said meekly...
*you have opened my eyes...*

*Now I see that as long as you are important you will have to defend yourselves...*

*as long as you are important, you will live in fear...*
*as long as you are in fear, you will need to scare others...*
*as long as you are you, you will have to prepare every moment for the future...*

*And, I also see that you are important...*
*in you I see a well-read, clever and successful adult... in you I see amazing books, well-crafted beliefs... in you I see all your past, your politicians, your newsreaders and your traditions...*

*I can see that all your fears are justified... and I will never question them again...*

*I can see how important you are... a lot has gone into making you, you...*

*How could I even question your fears... they are as real as you are...*

He apologised, as he slowly got up and left...

Strange guy I thought, that was 15 minutes wasted... which I could have just used worrying about my own stuff!

Disclaimer: The characters in the story are fictional, almost as fictional as your 'self' and its fears.

*Four*

FAREWELL

What died with you, were my expectations...
what died with you, were my desires...
what also died, were my future conversations with you...
and no more is the comfort, that you could provide...

What didn't die... is my love for you...
love lives on...
it is becoming stronger each day...

What didn't die, is your wisdom, and the things I learned being around you...
my lessons will be more treasured now...

What didn't die, is my gratitude, for having you in my life...
my gratitude will keep on growing each day...

I will reach that place soon, where I will be left with just love and gratitude...
and nothing else, in my heart, when I think of you...

I can see that day already, and I can smile today...
for being so fortunate to have you as someone so close to me...

You will not be missed... if I could carry forward even a little part of who you were...

And I will...
I will carry forward, the love you shared with all and everyone...
I will carry forward, the faith you had...

You will not be missed... if I remember what I learned today...

And I will...
I will remember, that love and gratitude are the threads, with which I need to relate to each person in my life...

Because, these are the few things, which outlive all endings... my love my gratitude and my lessons...

May god give me strength, to act on this wisdom even in tough times...

May god give me strength, to let go of my unfulfilled desires, expectations and dreams which I had for you...

Now that you rest, I want you to rest...

Time passes fast... and I will be where you are... very soon... and I know I will see you smiling as always!

Farewell my love!

# *Five*

## SELF, DOUBT AND FAITH

*S*elf! The mysterious one...
he had nothing of his own, and had no substance...
but he was good at presenting himself, and was master
of trickery...

He presented himself as many things, and was always
popular...

He lived like a celebrity, in his world...
nobody ever questioned him... they questioned everything under the sun but never him...

The secret of his success was that nobody had time
to find out who he really was... and all his acts were
appreciated...

For example, his act of love was quite popular...

he came dressed as love, and people always fell for it...
he said you can't go wrong with me because I am love...
and my whole life is the practice of love...

One day, when he was performing the act of love, lightning flashed... and people could see his designer garment... his garment was designed by lust... the color of his garment was jealousy... and it also had these huge pockets, called need...

They all saw it... they paused, they looked at each other, but nobody said anything...
nobody wanted to spoil the game... and his act continued...

Towards the end, this act had scenes of hatred, possessiveness, frustration, confusion, stress, loneliness and disgust... but people were told to expect these scenes as part of love...
this is how Self had played it for ages...
this must be by design, they always thought...

Another of his acts, was called piousness...
where he used to come dressed as a pure man and people loved him... he looked really serene and peaceful... he wore this perfect white robe which was whiter than anyone else's... he had this charming smile on his face, and people always fell for it...

One day as he performed, the lighting flashed once again... and, his white garment was so thin that people

could see underneath... and they could see that he wore the undergarments designed by pride, and yes there were pockets too, only they were sewn inwards...
again they paused, they looked at each other then looked away... the play went on...

There were so many other popular acts he performed... like the one of friendship, which used to start with the promise that it would never end, but always ended when they least expected it to end...

And the other one of giving, which was always a sell out amongst the intellectuals... It used to start with Self pretending to give stuff, and used to end with the scenes of Self making the other feel guilty of receiving...

[It is a story of a lifetime, to understand his acts... I know, even you don't have time for that... let's move on...]

Self's best friend and partner in his business was **Doubt**...
Doubt worked with him faithfully, he was always with him... he used to watch every single thing which was happening around Self...
Doubt had this nature of trusting no-one...
he always countered all beliefs of others, and was a sharp master of his art...
Self used to love Doubt, and he used to take Doubt's help all the time to suppress his critics...

And then there was **Faith**, this girl who was so in love with Self...

She was always near where Self was... theirs was a well-known love story... they used to live together years ago...

They were in love...
she loved him even when he was a nobody, and they were so complete when together... things fell apart when Self moved out in search of greater things...

But Faith never gave up on their relationship...

Now that Self had moved on... he found it quite annoying to have Faith trying to show her face all the time... he started using Doubt to make sure that Faith never entered his theatre...

But Faith was always around... always sitting outside his theatre, waiting for the acts to finish...

Doubt used to shoo her away in disdain, and never used to let her get a glimpse of Self...

Then one day, something really strange happened...

That day, when Doubt went to tell Faith to go away, for one more time... lightning flashed...

Doubt could see her eyes so clearly...
they reflected something strange...
something, he had never laid his eyes upon...
what is this, he thought...
he turned around in shock...

And for the first time ever... he laid his eyes on Self...

Self was shocked to see Doubt looking at him... he felt uncomfortable and annoyed, but couldn't say anything... he tried to continue his act... but it was so hard to perform with Doubt staring at him...

Faith smiled in joy... and she left that day...

Something in her knew, that now, Self will find her...

He will cross deserts if he has to... he will cross the river of fire if he has to...
but he will find her!

Epilogue
Doubt now faces towards Self, and Self is no longer having fun in his acts...
Faith is hopeful as ever... she still waits for Self...
her love is the type that can wait forever...

*Six*

## Seeking a stranger

*I*t was one of those non-special days...
and I was doing nothing special...

That day, a stranger came to meet me...

How different he was, than all what I had seen before...
and how joyful I felt that he was there...

His presence made time fly...
his presence took over everything that I was...
maybe even my heart stopped beating... because I can't
remember a beat, during the time he was there...

His presence made me wonder, if I could have him
forever...
I am not really sure what happened then...
I think he heard my thoughts... or did he sense 'me' being there... and he left...

But, I was happy even after he left...
I still felt that I was special... because he had come to me... so there was this bounce in my step, when I got out that day...
that bounce remained there for a long time...

Many months passed...

Now I didn't even remember what I was actually doing, when I met him...
or how he looked etc. etc.
but my desire to talk about him to others, made me fill the gaps in my story...
and I continued to talk about him for many more months...
with each description, I added little more glory to my story... hoping deep down that I would meet him again, and then everything would be fine...
I would reconcile all stories then...

But when I didn't see him for few years, I was a bit worried...

Maybe my doubts about his falseness were real... maybe they were right who laughed at my story...

Just to be sure, I started asking around...
I asked around if anyone has seen such a person...

I thought it would be easy to find him...
because no one can possibly miss him...

I was right, many people knew him...
I got many stories about his coming and his going...
people described how beautiful he was and how com-
forting he was...
and how uplifted they felt after meeting him...

But, to my surprise, not a single person could tell me
how to find him...
it is not that they didn't try... some said sit like this and
eat this & this and he would come...
I did everything they said, and yet there was no sign of
him...

Some said don't worry about him, only then will he
come... now this one was the most absurd suggestion of
all... I mean how I could possibly not worry about him
with an aim to find him...

Somebody even said "I am that"... very funny...

So frustrating to look for him...

But I haven't given up...

There is still no end to the ways which people tell me
to find him...
there is so much to be done, and I have become so busy
these days... but I am still trying...

Sometimes I think he doesn't exist...
and I deluded myself on that non-special day...

or, maybe he is trying to tell me that he is the big guy here, and not me... so, it is he who would decide when to come and go... who does he think he is...?

I would show it to him when I find a way to reach him... I would then reach him when I want... and I will tell the whole world how to reach him...

In the meantime, I study everything he left behind...
it is so, so tiring sometimes...
the only good news is that I have narrowed him down to few names...  people say he is called Peace, Happiness, Bliss or Love...

The list is so short now... I am so close...

I will find him!

PS:
Sometimes I long for that non-special day... when I was doing nothing special... and was not looking for anything special.

# *Seven*

## RELATING TO LIFE

*T*here is never a day, when I not need your touch...
there is never a day, when I not appreciate your
sounds...
there is never a day when you are not important...

Like a moon without the sun... I can be, but I can't
shine... without you...

There is never a day when I wish you to be different...
there is never a moment when I want to question you...
you are perfect as you are...

Like water becomes the pot, it's me who lives to take
your shape...

Every day, I wait for your warmth to finish me...
every day, I look forward to face the heat...
and to burn something I hold dear...

Like a drop of dew relates to the sun... I relate to you... to be evaporated bit by bit...

There is no place where I am hidden from you... there is no place where I can remain who I am... wherever I go, I face a challenge to change... you keep showing me my own image...  just the darker version of it...

Like a shadow you are... and how thankful I am to have the shadow...

I will never try to avoid you... I will never run away from you... I will never be scared of you... because I know, all you want, is to finish the 'me'... I will face you in all situations... I will even run towards you at times when you hurt the most...

Like a moth towards the flame... I will come to you, to live the end, and find a beginning...

If I need anything from you... I will be as gentle as I can... and touch as gently as I can... I will wait for the moment when my touch troubles you the least...

Like a butterfly takes from a flower... that is how I will take from you...

I see your compassion, when you hurt me... I know you love me, and just want me to find love...

I know you, and you know me even better...
I won't give up on you until you are... and you won't give up on me until I am...

It's like you are me, and I am you...

We love and we play...
I get frustrated and I get hurt... you get furious and you look ugly...
I get happy and I dance... you look beautiful and you give comfort...

So much happens between us...

And yet, there is never a me... and there is never a you!

# *Eight*

## One-sided love

*M*any times upon a time, there was a woman called Knowledge...

She was a curious woman who wanted to know it all... see it all... and understand it all...

She didn't care about anything, or, anyone other than herself... she did it all, for her own sake...

And yet, what fascination this man had for Knowledge... he used to follow Knowledge everywhere... he used to call her 'his' Knowledge...

He had travelled across the world following her... he had chased her from mountains to valleys... he had chased her in caves, on mountains and in homes...

He used to carry all her belongings on the way...
he used to treasure things she left behind...

Although, the bag became heavier each day, but he never slowed down or stopped following her...
his search seemed never ending... and his love for her seemed undying too...

Sometimes he would get frustrated arranging things in the bag full of her belongings...
the bag had it all... but, every-time it was too late before he found what he needed from that bag...

It was hard to find the right thing in that bag... forget about finding the right thing at the right time...

But he couldn't let the bag go either, because he was scared thinking what he would need when...
after all, none of it was useless, that he carried... he thought so...

And what else could he do, other than following her?
he didn't know anyone who could be trusted other than his Knowledge...
he was very, very lonely that way...
always, only trusting his Knowledge but, sadly his Knowledge was never his...
but, this love of his life was his only hope...
so he always found strength to get up and walk behind her...

Today, yet again, he felt like giving up the chase...

he can see that Knowledge is making him go in circles...
his head is hurting with the burden of her belongings...
the more he follows her the further she appears to be...

He needed rest from the chase... he stopped for a moment... sat down, and his eyes couldn't stay open...

Soon, he was dreaming of a place where he is with Knowledge...
a place where he is not confused, because he has Knowledge by his side...
he can even find the right thing at the right time because the bag only presents what is needed in the moment...
and he can feel the joy of having Knowledge walk with him, and not ahead of him...

He smiles in his sleep...
...

While he slept, Knowledge never stopped... she is walking fast...

Sun will be setting soon... again...

She is passing this village... and she can hear people talking about a man...
they were saying this man is setting an example of love, for all to see...
this man who loves a woman to death...
the man who follows his love across the mountains and valleys, and never gives up...

She is in awe of this man and wishes she could know him too...
She wishes that she can find him one day...
maybe she will... if she continues to travel, she thought...
she only knows how to walk faster and faster... she doesn't know that something important can be found... just by stopping...
she sighs!! and starts walking faster than before...
...

He suddenly wakes up... he has been dreaming for a while...
he needs to catch-up...
he hasn't lost her, he can see her shadow in the distance...
he starts walking faster...
he has been doing it for so many years... he will be fine...

Many times he has felt that she runs only because he chases...
but he can't stop either... he is too scared to be left behind...

Many times upon time he has chased her...
knowing deep in his heart, that once upon a time they were together...

One day they will meet...

For now, it is just him, and his one-sided love!

# *Nine*

## SELF, DOUBT AND FAITH - II

*A*fter that day, Self could never perform his acts with same intensity...
he was not used to Doubt facing towards him...
didn't he train Doubt to always face the world and not him?

It is painful... his acts are no longer popular... maybe deep down his acts have stopped fooling him too...

Doubt questions him every day, and Faith is nowhere to be found either...
there is just this empty theatre... no actor, no act, and no one to watch...

Silence, darkness, loneliness and despair is what is left...
he just wants to go back to the place where he lived so peacefully with Faith...

He needs to find her if he has to feel complete...

Doubt thinks he is responsible for what has happened...
he realises that it was him who first introduced Self
to the world of theatre a long time ago, when he questioned the value of his love...
at that time he had said 'you can be so much more, and
why are you wasting your life with this girl'...

Now, Doubt just wants these lovers to meet again... he
can't see the pain of his friend anymore...

Self and Doubt have started the long journey together
to find Faith...
they will soon find her...

Doubt helps him by questioning his pride, his ego, and
his beliefs at each step... and Self goes deeper and deeper within to find his truths...

Self often gets glimpses of that place where he used to be...
his thirst is increasing as the days pass...
somehow, nothing else seems to have meaning now...

Faith knows where they are...
she wants to run and embrace Self...
but it is not in her nature to interfere in his journey...
she loves Self too much...
she can't make him feel that she found him...

She wants Self to get that credit!

# *Ten*

## DEFINITIONS

*S*on, daughter, husband, wife, dad, mom, friend, noble, kind, rude, needy, greedy, clever...

Our definitions and our expectations of people come as masks in so many shapes and sizes...

Some try to run away, but sooner or later they get a mask too... a rebel, a gipsy, a spiritual seeker, or crazy if nothing else fits... after all there is a mask for everyone...

And, once you have a mask...
it is no longer about you...
your definition becomes bigger than who you are...
your definitions justify people's demands on you...

But, it is not all their fault...
you love your definitions too...
you take pride in your definitions...

you take pleasure in cursing those who don't fit their definitions...
you wear your definitions as collars on your neck and then you wonder what suffocates you...

Suffocation is not in the definitions, it is in your constant desire to put definitions above life...

Definitions have their place, they help you relate and feel secure in your relationships... but their place is behind life, not ahead of it...

The problem is not calling someone a loving person... the problem is hating the person the day he/she is not loving enough...

The problem is not calling someone Christian, Muslim, Hindu or Buddhist... the problem is when you kill that person, just for that reason...

The problem is not calling your loved one a husband or wife... the problem is you hating them when they don't behave like one...

Wear these definitions as shoes, and not as collars around your neck... you are always bigger than your names... because you came here first... and, your names came later...

Likewise, the other person comes in your life first, and your definitions follow later... so, let the person remain first when you relate, and let definitions remain second...

When in the business of relating to a living being, be prepared to be surprised... and, if you hate surprises, please fall in love with the dead...

You struggle to measure the mass of a particle in motion, and you want to relate to a human being based on your measure of him/her...
you will never be able to judge a life in motion...

Let the painting finish, before you define and frame it...
you are a work in progress and so is the one you hate or love...
let the painter work... learn to be quiet and watch...
learn to be amazed not angry when it looks bad...
learn to be grateful not pompous when it looks good...

Stop seeing persons, instead see and feel living beings...
when you judge, they feel little, because they are alive...
when you ignore, they get hurt, because they are alive...
when you are rude, you make them cry, because they are alive...
when you get angry, they get scared, because they are alive...

Stop hurting in the name of definitions...

Stop killing in the name of names...

Keep your definitions in your text books, and let them define what is dead...

Let your love guide you, when it comes to the living!

# Eleven

## I am Calmness

It is a miracle...
we are listening to calmness today...

So many thoughts and so much to worry, and yet, it is so, so quiet... as you listen to calmness...

Universe may be thanking you right now, for your attention...
you are at the centre of the universe as you listen to calmness...
...

I am calmness...

Have you ever thought about me...

Do I have any place in your priority of things...

Or, is it all about making sure that this should be like this, and that should be like that...
...

I am always there, waiting for your attention...

But I won't be seen, until you find the eyes to see me...

You will have to pay attention to little things to reach me...
...

A little patience, in handling the mistakes of others...

A little care for the other, who is no better than you... and definitely no worse than you...

A little appreciation for the sounds around you... and a little thought of the silence when it is really noisy...

A little pause before you judge... and a little time looking at the other, before you shout...

A little hesitation before you make your point... and a little smile, when you lose an argument...

A little patience when you feel hurt... and a little gratefulness for being alive...
...

Just little things... and you will find me...
...

Indeed a miracle... that you are with me, even now...
...

You can be with me, you see...
and you like being with me...
I wonder, why you wait for a break from life to find
me...

Why not take me to the busiest times of your day...

Why not drive with me, in your traffic jams...

Or walk with me, to lunch...

Why not spray me on your neck in the morning...
so that your words carry my fragrance during the
day...
...

Put me in your to-do-list tomorrow...
and I will take you through the day as if it was extended
morning...

In an argument you will hear the chirping of birds...
and behind the clouds of uncertainty you will see the
morning sky...

Just give me a look... once in a while... I am always waiting...

I only know how to wait...

I am calmness!

# Twelve

## MORE OR LESS

I am Mr. Shallow More!

This is what I bring -

More shouting, with less communication...
More communication, with lesser meaning...
More texting, with lesser messages...

More tools, with less utility...
More sex, with less love...
More years to life with less joy...
More choices with lesser options...

I am the consumer!

I wanted more of the good things...

But now, I realize... that more of a good thing... somehow makes the thing less good...

Thanks for what you have given Mr. Shallow More... maybe now, I will listen to Mr. Meaningful Less, a bit more.

# Thirteen

## ANGER

*L*et me begin the reading with a short story...

*A salesman asked a little boy playing outside a home - is your mother home?*
*The boy said – yes she is!*
*Salesman went ahead and knocked on the door... there was no response.*

*So he knocked a few more times, but still when there was no response he got a little frustrated.*
*He went and asked the kid again, is your mom really home? He said – yes, yes! She is definitely home, and continued playing.*

*The salesman went back and started knocking on the door harder. He also tried to listen for any sound coming from the house, but he could not hear anything. After banging the door a few more times, he was sure that there was no one inside.*

*He was furious at the kid; he went back and started shouting at him.*
*What's wrong with you? Why couldn't you tell me the truth? When no one is home why did you make me bang the door so many times? And I asked you twice didn't I?*
*The kid who looked shocked, replied... Listen sir, it is true that my mother is home. But this is not my home!*
*...*

You can laugh at the salesman, but this is how all your anger is... the result of misinformation in your head...

The secret to being angry... is to have fixed ideas about reality, and then realise that reality doesn't match your ideas...

Anger comes as a friend to help you fix reality...
he says, he is here to solve your problems, and promises to fix other people for you...
not only do his promises of fixing the world fail... but also, there is a lot, that he takes in return for his promises...

You just don't pay enough attention to the deal which anger brings...

When anger visits you next time...
ask him - what benefits do you bring, my friend?

What benefits, other than a momentary satisfaction of being proven right...?
or, may be some attention from those, I seek attention from...
or, may be a sense of being important and righteous...
or, maybe the kick of making the other feel guilty, so that I appear a better person...

Now weigh what he brings, against what he takes away...

He takes away exciting mornings, lively afternoons, joyful evenings and peaceful nights from your life...
while you burn in anger, you just miss them completely...

Weigh your lists, and then look at anger again...

Maybe you will give up your anger, for once...
for the sake of one evening...

For a change, be in the business of love and peace...
change the currency you have been using to buy attention, respect and love...
you can't buy respect and love using anger and control as your currency...

Next time you are writing an invitation letter to anger, just pause...
pause and look at a tree, or a bird, or the sky, or ground, or yourself in the mirror...

I am not asking you to forgive the other...
I am asking you to stop much before...
much before you reach the place, where you have to forgive the other...

Stop and ask what it is about... and, what is so wrong...

If you are angry because you are insecure...
then think why did you leave the womb when you had no insurance... no bank balance... no strength...
relax, if life took care of you then, it will take care of you tomorrow as well... and never feel insecure about things, which came as a gift without asking in the first place...

If you are angry because the other is not behaving as he/she should...
just think, are you behaving the way you want to... are you finished with your own flaws, so you now have time to fix someone else...
bring your energy back into helping you transform...

If you are angry thinking that you are right...
then know that if you were really right, you wouldn't be the one burning...

If you think it is your love for the other that makes you angry... then wonder whether light can be used to darken a room...

Decision is up to you...

Ignore a morning, or ignore a fault of the other...

Feel the energy of an afternoon, or enjoy the heat of an argument...

Enjoy a joyful evening, or make sure the other can't enjoy it too...

Go to bed with peace or with heartache...

Forget this reading as soon as it is over...
or, remember to question anger every time it visits you!

# Fourteen

## REST

$\mathcal{L}$et me finish this task...
let these months be over...
and then, I will find rest...
I am busy, this is not my time and place to seek rest...
...

How much will it take, before you realize, that it is your mind which doesn't know how to rest...?

Rest is not in the future, and rest is not on a beach or a mountain... rest is in the mind... a mind which does not know rest, will find turmoil even in a spa...

Rest is in a mind, which knows that there is no tomorrow...
that mind does not look for rest in future...
it just rests...

It rests in the knowledge that no matter how much I plan, tomorrow will never see the light of the day... it will always be this day, here, now...

You don't need to disengage from the world to rest... you just have to disengage from this treadmill called self... and you will find rest...

Unrest is the nature of a mind that is engaged with self... rest doesn't come to a mind that is busy with thoughts of making it good for 'self' someday... somehow... anyhow... a mind which is touched by each praise and blame...

Rest is not about being idle either... it is about being able to act from a place of rest within... an ability to have a mind which is at rest when reacting to the world...

If a thought tells you that rest needs a certain kind of place, and a certain kind of day... then that is a limiting thought... and, it will forever limit your capacity to rest...

Don't you see that you cannot rest in a place, which does not exist... and that you cannot relax at an hour that never comes...

The only place and time that exists, and is real, is here and now...
if you must rest; rest here, rest now...
and rest in each now, when life is at its busiest...

If you want a perfect retirement then retire from the process of wanting...
you will have a retirement villa with a view of the land-scape called Life...

Start investing in that retirement home today...
day by day, brick by brick build that retirement place of yours...
your every action and every thought can become an investment in your retirement...

Don't wait for a time to rest...
acquire a mind which can rest...

Don't just sit there...

Rest!

# Fifteen

## THE TEMPLE

Temple, is the space occupied by the divine...
    your body is a temple too, and its occupant is the
divine...

Like a temple is not visited for its décor, no one true of
heart, visits you because of your body...

Those who come for the shining exterior, are the merchants of paint...
they are the ones, who never cared about the deity
within...
the ones, who will disappear at first sign of a crack in
the walls...

Pure in heart, are those who are in love with the deity...
they come to pay tribute to the 'you' which is within...
the ones, who will be there even when the walls of your
temple are shattered and old...

Don't just be busy with the merchants of paint who come and go... take care of those, who never came for business with you...

And when you think about this temple of yours... think of it as a device of the divine...
it is to express the beauty within, and gracefully express it must...
so take very good care of it...
do it not because 'it' matters, but, because what it contains matters...

It contains the possibilities of greatest expressions of the universe itself...
it contains your most valuable asset and that is 'you'...
it is the only way you touch existence...
it is your only existence...

But, never ignore the deity within... take care of the whole if you seek health...
health is not just the absence of diseases...
health is about forgetting that you have a body...

It is not health enough when there is no pain, but your thoughts are about the body...

It is not health enough if you eat and sleep well, but you are always noticing people noticing your body...

Like a headache causes you to notice your head... when you notice the body a lot, it is a sign that there is a pain... why would you notice otherwise...

To arrive at health, work needs to be done on the whole...
your body, your mind, and your soul...

Your soul is the reason the body is here...
and when your soul comes in sync with its purpose...
your body starts laughing too...

When your body has perfect curves, any ugly top and jeans make you look good...
and when your soul sings any 'body' feels beautiful...

For perfect looks, a perfect body with less expensive clothes & makeup is enough...
for perfect body, a dancing soul filled with some love and compassion is enough...

You don't have to be tall or short or dark or fair or wide or thin...
you just need to be in good shape within, to begin with...

Your body is your tool, and you are not alone with a tool...
your tool is not better or worse than the other... it is just different...

just pots of different shapes & colors made of the same clay...

If you have put hours of sweat & paint to shine your pot...
then just be thankful that you could... don't let it judge those who haven't...

Pots are all beautiful as they are...
no one pushes you to look good I hope...
and you shouldn't make someone feel less, just because they can't match your fitness routine...
just shut-up and mind your own body...

If you've got the best, then don't be proud...
no one will remember you for your curves and pecs for more than a month...

If you've got the worst, then don't feel ashamed...
isn't it enough to just have one in the first place... isn't it enough to just be here, and, experience life...

Finally, as you learn to take care of your temple...
let this remain in the back of your minds...
that this temple of yours...
will not be there forever...

'Temp' in temple, says it all!

# Sixteen

## DEATH OF A SPIRITUAL SEEKER

There must be something else, he thought!

What he saw in life was not good enough to consider living for even one more day...
if he had to live, he needed to be something else, he needed to be more...

There must be light... because he could see the shadow; the dark shadow, which fell upon everything from relationships to health, and made his world look like such a hard place to live... for shadow to be there; three things were needed, the light, the obstacle and the surface on which it falls...

The surface was the world around him... but what is the obstacle and where is this light?
or is the shadow of suffering an illusion?

There must be an answer... because he could feel the flames of his questions...
there must be water, because he could feel the thirst...

And for years the cycle went like this:

He found the pride of knowing, practicing and being on the path which is so worthy...
and, he hid the pain of not really knowing anything...
he thought, if the whole world thinks I know, then they must be right... moreover, who cares if I don't know as long as they don't know that I don't know... and, thus so-called learning went on...

He also found the pleasure of control and righteous-ness... but he suffered in the agony of knowing that control was an illusion... and that righteousness always left him the very moment he needed it the most...
but again, who cares as long as I look righteous, he thought... isn't that all that matters... he continued falling... but kept on learning to get up before anyone noticed...

He enjoyed the intellectual circus and knew many tricks...
as he performed, he knew that there is no safety net to hold him if he falls... so he was always doubtful and shivering inside when he made his claims... who cares, he thought, as long as people clapped... we all die one day, so why not make the most of the admiration, as long as it lasts...

Years passed...
and now he sits alone in a dark night...
he has had enough of following everything that was sold as good... he has had enough of society, science, philosophy, religion, retreats, courses, books, methods, and all the rest of it...
the whole circus of seeking solutions and of living a life...

He has had enough of the remedies and claims made by well-dressed monks...
he has had enough of the fake smiles & hollow promises...
he had seen the miserable face of what goes on, in the name of love for the other...
he had seen suffering justified by formulas and beliefs...
he had seen freedom dressed in golden chains claiming to be free...
he had seen the stoned face of success...
he had eaten the magic pills for happiness too many times... felt like throwing up...

He felt lost; it was not his life anymore, he thought... his search, the single thing worth living for, didn't really solve anything...
he couldn't move forward or go any further in any direction...

He knew his thirst is real and there must be water... he can't find the lofty ideals of beauty in the world, and yet, he knows that the world cannot be dark everywhere he goes... because darkness would not have felt dark, if there was no light anywhere ever... and that the pain would not feel so painful, if he was made of pain...

But what more can he do...
he has had enough of believing, wanting, practicing, non-practicing...
he gives up...

Suddenly, the path came to an end...

He could never find a solution...
no questions were answered...
no tears, no funeral, just a sudden end...
...

There is another person though, who now lives!

One who doesn't seek... one who doesn't need to find... he is forever wondering and smiling... playing and dancing... floating not swimming... feeling not holding... moving but not going anywhere...
loves but is not in love with a thing... belongs but never stays... sings but it is not his song...

Someday, you too may find that person, he hopes...
...

There is a new beginning waiting at the edge of each end...

Find the end, if you seek the beginning!

# Seventeen

## LOVE & LOVE+

*I* am love!!!

I bring immense pleasure to begin, but I don't stop there...

I bring strong attachments, to make it hard for people to leave...

I bring fierce jealousy, to ensure that no one dares to tell the truth...

I bring strong possessiveness, so no one dares to smile too much...

I bring firm commitment, so that a relationship is sealed and secure...

I bring complete social recognition and support, so that no one doubts me...

I bring so many pre-defined, pre-packaged and tiresome special days & events too...

And, to top it all, I bring out-of-this-world promises, expensive gifts, and lots of them...

Who are you? What do **you** bring?

I am Love+...
I bring myself... and then, even I am not there.

# *Eighteen*

## THE SECRET

*I* cannot tell you the secret...
no one can, and ever has...
telling a secret, defies the definition of the secret...

The secret doesn't remain a secret once told...
and the secret of the universe never works when you
learn and use it like a formula...
because what you know or can know is not a secret...
even if one person knows it, it is not the secret anymore...

For a secret to remain secret, and work like a secret, no
one should know it, including you...

That is how the secret of the universe works... by re-
maining beyond our understanding forever...

What becomes known and understood, is not the secret
of the universe, it is your own personal entertainment...

so let's burn all that makes you think you have the secret...

The secret does work, but only for those who don't look for secrets...
because they are too busy being engaged with their passion... universe takes care of them... secretly...

There is no formula, hidden or known, other than changing the person, who is looking for a formula...

You can try to learn love, you can try to learn kindness, you can try and talk to the universe, you can try and send positive signals... but none of it works, as long as the source is corrupted... you cannot make a room brighter with a broken lamp... fix the lamp, and light will shine...

Do not ever look to arrive at a place, where you know... you will never be there, because you are life... your way is flowing forever...
let flowing and constantly learning, remain your journey...
being knowledgeable is imaginary and harmful...

You may never know the secret...
but if you keep learning with life... the secret will know you... and take care of you...

The universe never listens to what you say, want or do... secretly, the universe, always, just knows who you are... it just keeps giving you what belongs to who you are... and just keeps putting you at a place, from where you can change who you are...

There is no secret shortcut to cheating the system... a method, a book, a practice is just a beginning, the real work is to change the being...

You don't expect even your boss to raise your salary without reason... how do you expect that the most intelligent of all... the sum total of entire existence, will suddenly transform your life, without you becoming worthy of that transformation...

If the secret could be contained in a formula, we would have created Bachelors of love, and Masters of awakening, in our universities, long before now...

Stop looking for secrets... start working on the obvious...

Stop practicing visions... have a vision... and, follow your vision, like there is no tomorrow...

Stop practicing love, start loving...

Stop practicing the art of communication, start caring, when you talk...

Stop praying for the world; change the world - one person at a time... and, begin with yourself please...

And that... is the only secret...
the well-known secret...
worth knowing again, and again!

Shush!

# Nineteen

## LOVERS, FREEDOM AND MARRIAGE

### Part - I

Slowly, she turned around...
and his heart caught a new rhythm...
as she turned to look at him, he felt as if he saw the
complete ascent of the moon in that single moment...

Her heart too, skipped a beat or two...
In that moment, she just knew what she needed to be
complete...

They kept talking for hours that day...
it was him, she was sure... and why not,
he said his name was prince, and his last name was
charming...

Soon their hearts were in sync...

in sync with the rhythm of life... now nothing would ever separate them...
nothing else would ever matter again, they thought... they both fell... in love of course...

Everyone said they were perfect...
you could see it in their eyes, it was hard to believe that they had just met each other...
their souls seemed made for each other, and they could not stop looking at each other...
they could not think of anything but the other... they were just perfect together...

*Time,* was flying fast...

As it is with things in love... they too had a place of their own...
it was not a palace, it was small, but, it was their own...
that place used to make them feel like they were a prince and a princess...
they were always in this place, those days...
this place was nowhere, but, was theirs to use in all places...

In this place they also had a bird, which they both loved...
this bird was a reason for their joy since they met...
this bird was called Freedom...

She was the bird of the wild - untamed, undisciplined, uncultured...

they had found this bird when they first met, under that tree of joy on that sunny afternoon...

It was all perfect...
and, they decided that they would make sure that they will never ever lose that place...
many times, they promised each other to never lose what they have today...

*Time,* was still flying fast...

One day, they were both sitting together, hand in hand, with Freedom nearby... they looked and, felt rich... because they didn't need anything else...

As it is with things that are rich, they too had many unwanted followers... one of them was this man called society... he visited them once again that day... they welcomed him like a friend...
they used to trust him, because he always gifted them nice things...
he used to come and protect them when needed,
he used to provide all sorts of comforts to them... most of the times he used to give them things, without being asked... magically, he seemed to know what they needed and used to come and sell it to them...
and, of course, he was genuine... he said so...

Today, he came by, to sell them a special bird... a well-trained, highly disciplined and well-respected bird... this bird was called Marriage...

She was a very popular bird...
he didn't have to do too much selling, lovers knew all about the bird...
they knew this bird comes with a promise of everything, which they were looking for...
it was such a good deal they thought...

They told everyone about the purchase and everyone supported them...
people even contributed some money towards the purchase...
how nice of people, they thought, they all just want us to be happy...

They bought the bird and couldn't stop smiling about the deal...
and, because that man always knew better... he sold them cages too...
he knew, that each bird should belong to a cage...
he also knew that each bird should have her own personal space... so they bought two beautiful cages, one for Freedom as well...

Now, they had each other, both birds and their lovely cages...
the world seemed perfect...

Isn't it great to be in this world, they thought...

They thanked everyone, and moved into a new place with the birds...

To live, happily ever after!

## Part-II

It was not even a day in the new place, when the lovers
started sensing discomfort...
they could see it in the eyes of both the birds...
things were not perfect with them...
the lovers could smell it in the air, but they couldn't
bother, they had a lot to do and look forward to...
and, fortunately it was not all bad...
both birds managed to agree in some matters, and
sometimes, were even seen playing together...


Months passed...

The play-time between birds was decreasing...
now they disagreed on most things...

Once the lovers overheard the birds arguing...

Freedom said 'things should be my way in this house,
because I came here before you, and anyways they both
love me more than you'...
Marriage, who was a sophisticated and cultured bird,
didn't shout like Freedom, but made her point very
clear... she said 'from now on it will be my rules which
will govern this place'...

Freedom couldn't understand why the lovers needed this new bird at all... and she couldn't see what was lacking in their lives before Marriage came...
and Marriage couldn't believe that the lovers could be so dumb, to find joy, in the company of this untamed, uneducated fool, before she arrived...

The lovers felt torn between these two birds...
they sat together with both the birds and tried to fix things between them...
they said that they would make sure that neither of them felt the lack of love, and that they are both equally important...
they told Freedom to learn from Marriage and they told Marriage to appreciate Freedom...

Freedom believed them and hoped that things would be better someday...
but Marriage just smiled, she knew better... she knew that this is how it always starts...
she was confident that in the end, it would be all her rules in the house...

She was confident because she had very powerful friends in the bird community...
like Jealously, Beliefs and Control to name a few...

Freedom on the other hand didn't know anyone but Joy...
Joy was a fickle bird and didn't really care about who does what...

she only used to come when she felt like... so she was not much help...

Soon Jealousy, Beliefs and Control started to visit the house often...
and, this bunch started treating the house as their own...

As days passed, Freedom felt more and more suffocated... she used to be sad... :-(
she couldn't say anything, but she knew that Marriage was not doing the right thing...
she was bullied by the visiting birds each day... she used to hide as soon as they came...

Freedom knew that it wouldn't be easy for her in this house anymore...

*Time,* was still flying... but not so fast...

Years passed...

Freedom, now, became this bitter bird, who used to try and bite anyone who came near her... she used to cry, every time she was alone... she was not good company any more...

The lovers were now convinced that Freedom is stubborn...
they knew what needed to be done!

One day, they told Freedom that they want to let her go...

She was horrified!! Let me go where...? She thought... where could I possibly go, without them?

She started screaming... she was shaking within...
her tears were flowing...
and each drop, meant just one thing...
this is not how life was meant to be...

The lovers opened the cage... she didn't fly...
she couldn't move...
it was not that she wanted to live there any more...
she was just numb, to realise that she didn't want to live any more...

The lovers did not have time for any drama...
they picked her up... and took her to throw her where they found her...

As they were throwing her, they paused... a shiver passed down their spine...
it was a strange fear, which they felt in that moment...
but they both turned back, and left quickly, no time for strange thoughts, they thought...

And they went back to live with the rest of the birds...

Consistently ever after!

## Part – III

Years have passed...
feels like yesterday, when they moved in...

It is no longer the place, which the lovers dreamt of,
but, this is how it is supposed to be...

Isn't it...

People say they are doing well...

That man visits them in their moments of weakness...
he gives them a variety of drugs to cope with their troubles...

Freedom still waits for the lovers to come back...

*Time,* still flies... but now, it flies in circles...

Surprisingly, Marriage is not happy either...
although the lovers ask her for advice on all things, she
feels the lack of Freedom in the house...
she knows something is missing...

She hopes, that someday she and Freedom can live
together...
she prays that the lovers will go back to the day they
bought her...
on that day, they looked like the king and the queen...
things were so different for them... they shared their

souls, even when they didn't share the bed... it is no longer about them, with them... it seems more and more, about 'that man', she felt...

She no longer wants that man to visit the lovers, too often... he acts as if he knows it all... he sells with such confidence that the lovers keep buying his stuff...
the house has become cluttered...
it is full of formulas to make Marriage happy...

Only she knows, none of them worked...

It will be such a waste of a life, if what she saw, is as good as it will ever be...

She now wishes that her friends were different...
because she knows, nothing will change unless her ugly friends are kicked out...

She feels powerless... only the man and woman of the house can kick her friends out...

She can see she is in trouble... it shows in the lack of appreciation of lovers for her...
she can see herself being thrown out too...

She pinches herself every-day to see if she is real... she always thought she was real... but she can see herself disappearing everyday...

Is she a creation of that man who sold her to lovers...
to make sure that Freedom can be tamed...  that man
never liked Freedom...

She has tried to tell that man to look at things...
she has shouted in his courtrooms, and she has cried in
his bedrooms...

Maybe this time, she will ask that man to recreate her...
spray-painting of feathers that he has been suggesting,
has not worked at all... she wishes, she is born again
with new feathers...

That man sits somewhere in the distance... he knows
he didn't do anything wrong...
he just doesn't have time for complaints...
he is always too busy with fixing so many things for
the lovers...

But he can hear whispers... he overheard a few questions too...

What will happen to Marriage?
Will that man be able to recreate her?
Did the lovers need her in the first place?
What about her troublesome friends?
Who is going to kick out Jealousy from the house?
Who is going to give up Control?
Who is going to throw out Beliefs, that stubborn bird,
who wears dark glasses?

Will someone go and pick up Freedom from that place again?

He shook his head... He had a lot to get done and didn't have time to ponder over all this...
Lazy yapping people, he thought... and he continued working...

Marriage was seen flying away from the house, that night!


## Part - IV

This is what Marriage wrote to lovers, before leaving quietly that night:
...

Will you unburden the one you love... so that I can get my wings back and fly...

Will you seek to connect your hearts... so that I can sing on the cord, which connects...

Will you create space for me to sing and dance... or, will you continue to buy formulas and clutter the house...

Will you kick out the ugly birds from the house... or will you love Control, Jealousy and Beliefs more than me...

Will you set each other free... or, will you remain a policeman and a beggar, constantly watching the other and constantly asking from the other...

I know you will say that you can't take care of all this alone; and, that it takes two to make this work...

I also thought it takes two to make this work, when I was naive...

But now I have come to realise otherwise...

I know it needs two to make an argument work... it takes two to make a fight work...
but I also know, that it doesn't take two to make **love** work...
it doesn't take two to make **sacrifice** work...
and, it doesn't take two to make **kindness** work...

I have learned from what I saw, after I tied you together...
lo and behold! a miracle happened...

I joined one with one, and got - minus two!!

Now I know that the knot I used to tie you together, was not the right one... equation became thus: Not (me & you) = Not (me) + Not (you)... both, making sincere efforts, to not be themselves... two people who live together, but not in the same place...

I now know, if you continue to try and be Not(you), you cannot become an addition in a join...
you will always subtract from the other...
no matter how close you try to get to the other, you will keep walking away...

Her diary ends here.
...

Last we heard was Marriage is searching for a knot which doesn't tie people together, but which sets them free... which doesn't reduce, but adds to both...

A knot in the heart, which makes one sink when the other suffers... and, which makes one smile when the other laughs...

A knot, which tells them that now they are free...
because now there is someone to hold them, if they fall...

Now they can fly far, because, now there is a home to return to...

Now they have a place, where they can go back with the knowledge that, no matter how tired they are, they will be comforted... a place where no matter how unsuccessful they are, they will be respected... a place where no matter how they look, they will be admired... and, a place where no matter what emotion they carry, they will be loved... that place will be their own sweet little home...

Freedom is suffering a lot... she needs to be taken care of badly... she waits for the lovers to find her again...

The lovers are trying to find a balance; a balance in this house full of formulas and birds of different colours... they are ok... people say they are doing well... the thing working for them is that they are convinced that this is how it is supposed to be... they have forgotten the skies and are happy with the roof...

That man called society, is not bothered about petty questions of Joy and Freedom... he is still focussed on things which need urgent attention...
for example; that super effective hair gel, which will make a rat rook like a rabbit...
or, that drug which will make the old look young and the dead live a little longer...

*Time*, still flies... mostly in circles!

# Twenty

## THAT MAN

That man never wanted to become more important than joy and freedom...
it was never his plan...

He wanted to give the lovers better and safer places to live... easier access to food and water...
he wanted to help them organize their lives better... he wanted to ensure that lovers can be protected from the uncertainties of life...

He wanted to make life easy for them...
so they could focus more on finding love...

The lovers betrayed him...
somewhere along the way, they stopped focusing on love, and fell for the comfort and securities, which he brought...

It became a vicious cycle... due to his love for the lovers, he kept fulfilling their new demands...
and because each thing he brought was so attractive, they kept walking further and further away, from the pursuit of love...

He is sad today... because recently the lovers have started cursing him, for the lack of love they feel...

This is what he wrote to lovers today:
...

I am busy with tiresome meaningless pursuits because your wish is my command... and I exist for you...

I am yours in sickness and in health... forgive me today for yearning for health though...

I know I am sick, but I will not give up... I just cannot stop, until you stop asking for more...
even more than my diseases, I really feel sick about what I have become...

I get treated for one disease, and I see a new one developing next day...

The other day, I thought I fixed discrimination, but today, I found out that the infection has gone deeper in my skin...
and, when I thought I fixed hatred, I saw a lover killing many others for no real reason...

I feel even sicker, because all that I am doing for you, is not working for you either...

After I thought I got rid of your tears... I found that tears now hide as dry water behind your eyes...
and whenever I put a smile on your faces, it falls off, the moment you look away from each other...

I live on drugs, and stand as a patched up doll... but I will keep on walking...
I cannot give up... as I have you to serve... I am actually working harder, and harder, each passing day...

Trust me, I am not the villain in your story...
you have just decided to put your demands to me, above your own love...

I can't remember... but can you?? When did you stop focusing on love...?
I am also not sure where you learnt that freedom and joy, are not important for you...?

What sleep has overtaken you lovers, and, what dream, has caught your fancy...?

The night is getting darker, yet I have faith...
I have faith, because I can see a small flame in your hearts, which just won't go away...
it stands as the last argument of light in this dark night...

And I have hope...

I know the day you find the light in you... is the day it will be all fine between me and you...
darkness of a thousand years doesn't need thousand years to die... a flash of light and it will be gone...

I know you love your dream...
I know you are too busy...
I know it is so hard to remember the light right now...

But, I will be here... waiting and watching...

I will pray that you forget your pursuits... so that you can remember...
I will pray that you stop for a moment... so that you can arrive...

Wakeup, lovers... so that you can see a new dream!

Yours,
In sickness and in health

# Twenty One

## BEING YOU

$\mathcal{B}$eing you, is not easy... so many flaws and so much pain... the pain asks for revisions... and in each revision, you hide a flaw with another... pain changes face, and comes back...

But there is great hope... because you are here, now... and it all, always, starts here and now... your past has made you who you are now... your past has left you with so many scars and flaws... but your now, has power to destroy your past...

Just a little attention by you, to the process of sculpting a new you... and you will be renewed...

Just make sure, that you are watching you, at all times... and are fearless in accepting your flaws, and tireless in fixing them...

Don't rush to regret or say sorry... if you say sorry too quickly, you will be taking the easy path... flaws grow slowly, and they die slowly too... incubate your flaws with warmth of your scrutiny and understanding...
prepare yourself to let them go... by living in the pain of having a flaw for some time...

Don't rush to curse yourself for being a bad person either...
you are much bigger than the behaviors you exhibit...

Just the fact that you have started noticing a flaw, means that it will ripen and fall soon...
let it ripen, and then fall... so it doesn't leave you craving to go back...
a flaw, which is removed by understanding its pain...
never ever comes back to touch you...

Don't rush to the comfort zone of knowing that when something unpleasant happens through you, it is an aberration... it is never an aberration... it is the result of what you are... it is your own behavior which grew on you, over time... you have just thought of it as something good for you, till now...

The effort to understand your flaw, will teach you to accept yourself, for who you are...
and, it will make you forgive others whom you want to be different...

It may be easy to cover the flaw, and painful to uproot the flaw... or it may feel futile to remove a flaw, when it can be so easily hidden...

But, will you do the same if your flaw was a wound in your body... wouldn't you feel more and more pain, the longer you hide it... haven't you noticed how your frustrations become more and more painful each passing day...

Don't worry if you feel left behind as you work on yourself... while some are busy painting the exterior, you will be busy sculpting a new you...

You are not alone with the flaws...
and, you are not alone in your failures to remove your flaws... so never feel alone as you travel...

Being you, is the best you can do...
so, never feel bad, if it is not enough for the world... you, as you are, is enough for the universe, and it should be enough for you...

Being you is a journey, which no one else has ever undertaken... universe is watching your steps with great interest, for that reason... make it the best that you can...

Being you, is a blessing, savor it!

# Twenty Two

## Wonderful Sex

We have used sex, to forget our problems...
We have used sex, to make someone feel important...
We have gifted sex, out of pity...
We have participated in sex, as duty...
We have used sex, to release the sexuality gathered during our busy days...

We have had sex, in the hope that it will help a relationship...
We have had sex, to seal the deal of commitment...
We have had sex, to prove to ourselves that we are still young and fit...
We have had sex, to show that we are still passionate about each other...
We have planned sex, to have a child...
We have had sex, in the name of tantra, kundalini & enlightenment...

We have had sex, to feel victorious...
We have had sex, to gain personal favors...
We have had sex, because there is nothing else to do...
We have had sex, to end a fight...
We have had sex, to respect someone else's feelings, while disrespecting our own...
We have had sex, to quench our lust of someone other than the person in bed with us...
...

You may call all of the above sex, only due to a lack of another word... but, it is just another mundane activity...
...

Sex, in its purest form, is the physical expression of what your soul wants...

When your soul wants to dissolve with another, your body follows, and, tries to become one...

When your being is naked in front of someone, your clothes drop too...

When you surrender to the other, your body surrenders too...

When you want to give your whole being to someone, the body gives in too...

When sex happens as a prayer...
when sex happens as an answer, to a prayer...

when sex comes as an ultimate teacher of love...
when the act of sex transforms your being...
and when you can never ever be, who you were before
the act...

Then, that is sex - the beautiful feeling of watching the
boundaries of the self dissolve between two people...

By this definition, you can count on the fingers of your
hand, the number of times you would have had sex...

Don't be disheartened though... it is not as important to
have sex, as it is to know the beauty within you, which
it expresses...

To know that beauty, you must learn to wonder... and,
fortunately, there is a lot to wonder about...

Just wonder, how it has come to be the most hidden
of all our behaviors, and yet, the most visible of all our
expressions...

Just wonder, that despite this being the body's purest desire, it gets satisfied at times, in the most disgraceful ways...

Or wonder, why you love sex...
you don't seem to get anything, at the end of it...
you don't seem to change anything about yourself, by
engaging in it...

Or wonder, why you hate sex...

you don't hate eating and you don't hate drinking... is it because your parents and preachers have said so...

Or wonder, why you fear sex...
is it because every time you surrendered in sex, you were heart-broken later...
is it because sex destroys your beautiful friendship with the other person...

Or wonder, why you hide sex...
is it because deep down you know, that whatever you do in the name of sex, is not sex...
is it because it helps to keep sex more interesting than it actually is...
is it because you just want the sexual jokes to remain funny...

Or wonder, why sex is important to you...
is it because your magazines and therapists say it is so...
is it because you have nothing important to do and life is so mundane...
is it because everyone else says it is important...

Just wonder...

And admire the process which is your peak of human experience...

If you keep wondering... you will soon become wonderful... and the day you become wonderful, your sex will be wonderful too!

# Twenty Three

## LET'S NOT PLAY GAMES

*I*f you have ever loved a video game, you will know that solving a level in a game gives you a high; although, really, it gives you nothing more than the worthiness to play the next level...

But still you feel good...
the joy is not because of the game... it is because you are designed to play this way...

The only way to keep enjoying the game, is by continuously trying to solve the level you are in right now...
it becomes very, very frustrating when you have to fight the same fights again and again...
the frustration is because the essence of our being 'the warrior within', is not designed to be stuck at a level...
it is designed to rise above each situation, and to avoid falling into the same traps many times over...

Similarly, as we move through life, we must smile and welcome all things which force us to move to the next level... things, which force us to challenge our strongly held beliefs, traditions and habits, at our current level of existence...

Do not underestimate the power of these traps to resist change... just remember the only sacrifice you can make is, to sacrifice a bit of who you were yesterday... all the rest is just a trap and will keep you stuck on being who you are...

There is no key outside you, to help you in this game... all challenges are dependent on your character's unique place in time-space...
there is no one else playing the same game as you...

In the game within, there is no shortcut either... you have to solve level – 1, before you can solve level - 2...
you have to earn your right to solve the problem of misery and joy of the world, by solving your problems within first...
you have to earn the right to be able to help, by becoming free of your own agendas first...
you cannot yourselves be stuck at level - 1, where you are pulled and pushed by your own desires like a dry leaf, and, at the same time, try and help others to be free of their desires and expectations towards you...

The place where your game takes place, is within you... and, by this design, you don't reach the next level, until you kill some of your own villains within you...

Therefore do not try to solve or avoid your life-situations by using external solutions, or by watching ready-made dreams of future...

there is no future-distant place or situation, when you will magically be fine...

it's only by facing your 'now', and by being right 'here', you will have to earn the right to be fine...

A big reason of frustration in a life, is that at a certain level, you think you have 'arrived'... and have become who you are... a statement like "this is who I am, what can I do", is a sure sign of someone calling a certain level home and giving up on the game...

What you are today is not who you are... what you are today, is your actor's stage in the game... who you are, is the warrior behind the game... that warrior is not designed to be satisfied at any level...

Listen to your warrior, it keeps telling you through your negative mental states, that the making of you, is not done yet...

Don't ever, ever think that your negative states like anger, fear, jealousy or frustration are there because someone else did something... don't stop at this answer ever... it's a huge trap, and we have all fallen for this one, too many times...

For example, when my knee hurts, I don't think of putting balm on someone else's knee... I should not fight and dream about fixing the other person, when my head hurts in frustration, anger or jealousy...

Keep it simple - when your head hurts, your head needs the balm... you can try the balms of understanding and love... and if these don't work for you right now, find your own... just never try to stitch up the world, when the open wound is in you...

It is a tough remedy, but, it is the design - the design, which ensures that there is no end to how much you can learn in life... the design which ensures that either you move with the game, or suffer...

You have chosen to play... play like a warrior... make yourself worthy of the next challenge each passing day...
don't fall for old fights - the fights, which you have won and lost several times...
don't beat the person next to you, seek to beat the enemy within...

You see the necessity to win, but you have so, so many reasons to keep losing...

Stop playing games...

Be game enough to play!

# Twenty Four

## FAKER & SEEKER

*I* am the faker:

I can quote from the scriptures...
I have listened to mystics and I claim to understand them all...
I make regular announcements about my spiritual adventures...
and I know a few shortcuts to spiritual success...

I donate only what I have in excess, and, then I ensure that it is noted...
I master spiritual practices that are popular...
and I fight, to defend my beliefs if needed...

I have learned Yoga to feel better about me...
I do meditation and attend retreats to reduce stress...
I attend spiritual gatherings to talk about me...
I go to ashrams to forget who I am...

and I join tantric groups for sex and drugs...

Although, I am sometimes worried about me...
but, I am righteous, I am spiritual, and I am better than
you...

I am the seeker:

I wonder, who I am...
I wonder, why I am here...

I wonder, if I know...
I wonder, where I will go.

# Twenty Five

## SILENCE

*T*oday I will say just one thing...

## Twenty Six

## YOU AND WORK

*Y*ours is a strange friendship...
you have been meeting every-day, for so many years...
but, yet you get frustrated, and believe that Work is your problem...

You suffer on many days, thinking that you deserve your Work to be better...

Work knows that you don't enjoy his company so much...
he has been noticing the changes for some time...
and, this is what Work, wrote for you today:
...

All I know is that I never changed...
I didn't change, because I am not like your moods...

115

it was not long ago, when you were so excited to find me...
but look at you now, being dragged to me by some unknown force...

I am still that same old friend that I used to be...
I am still someone who looks forward to see you every day...
I still make sure that your needs are fulfilled...
I still provide for your family and you...
I still bring you opportunities to contribute...

I do understand your reasons for wanting to leave me, but can I ask for a small change in you, before you give up on us...

Don't worry, I won't ask you to change your looks...
I won't ask you to change the way you walk or talk...
I won't ask you to change your tools or methods...

Keep everything, as it is...
but, change this one thing...
change the way you see things...

1. Change the way you see problems... in them, see a situation, which is different from the picture in your mind... just re-align your mind to reality and it will tell you where to go from there...

2. Change the way you see mundane tasks... the tasks may be insignificant, but you are not... you are precious,

and tasks have value, because of you... it's not the other way round...

3. Change the way you see time... see it in heartbeats... a clock can tick forever... it can make you think you have endless time... but, heartbeats are limited, make sure none of them are wasted in hating what you do...

4. Change the way you see others... in them, see more of you; struggling to survive, just as you are... sometimes angry and worried just as you are... sometimes excited just as you are... work with them, as they try to work with you...

5. Change the way you see change... when you see pain in a process or a relationship... first, look at ways for more trust, wellbeing, openness and honesty as solutions... only then, look at your toolbox of processes...

I know you too want this relationship to work... and, I know you will find a way to change...

Because, I know there is something more than what you think, which brings you, to me, every day...

It is not my money, which brings you to me... because I know you for a long time...
I have seen you laughing more, when you had less...

Let me tell you what I think it is...

It is something that you have forgotten...
it is the thing, which made you jump after you finished
your first sandcastle... or made you scream in joy, when
you added color to a meaningless sketch...
above all, it is the search for that joy, which brings you
to me everyday...

Your joy lay in your contribution...
your joy lay in creating joy...

Go and find your unique way to contribute...
or, continue to seek favours from life, and be
disappointed...

Go, if you wish... stay, if you want...
but stop presenting half of you in return, when life presents a full day to you...

I hope you remember what I said today...
I hope you remember the right reasons for our union...
I hope you remember the child within - the child, who
wanted to make each sandcastle differently... even
though, they were all the same...
...

If you can find the passion to make a difference to what
you touch... then you and I will find a way through any
trouble we face...

Your contributions borne of joy, will add joy to the world... and for that reason, we will be protected by forces bigger than the share market...
forces, which create stars and make the world go round...
those forces are just in love with joy...
and, the real bottom-line of a human business is never a line... it is an upward curve, on human faces...

From now on, wakeup to create smiles and not sur-plus... wakeup to make a life, and not a living...
and, you will never find me tedious...

If you can remember the right reasons; then, ours will become a very special story...

Our story awaits... for you to remember!

Yours,
In excess and in dearth

# Twenty Seven

## JEALOUSY

*A* little green bird entered our house the other day...

What do you want from me, I asked...

*I just want to burn you from within, if you don't mind...*
*she said...*

Oh, why would I mind...? I am good at it...
it helps me divert my attention from the other issues,
which I am facing right now...

It gives me reasons to be less helpful, less compassion-
ate and less productive for the day...
It allows me to show others that I am full of love...
people see this fire in me as my love in most cases...

It allows me to threaten those, whom I think I love...
it makes them surrender all their smiles to me and me
only...
It gives me strong pain too, but, I am so used to it, and,
I know that the pain is for right reasons...
I am sure it is for right reasons, don't you think...

*Sure! She said and smiled... imagine what would happen
to me if you said that the pain is not for right reasons...
why will I even be here, in that case...*

Yeah! the pain is for right reasons, because when I love
someone, it makes perfect sense to feel pain if that person doesn't love me back... isn't that love...

*The bird just smiled mysteriously...*

And suddenly, it felt as if she was wearing my smile... I
couldn't find it on my face... it must be mine...

I wondered how this happened...

It happened when I used love to justify my fire...

How can my love for someone, justify the pain in me, I
thought...

How can my love justify the pain I give to the one I
claim to love...

I asked the bird... is it love or is it my insecurities that bring you here...

Or, is it my own desire to always remain the most important person around...

Or, is it my understanding that love means I am number one forever for my love...

Or, is it my firm belief that love hurts, that brings you here...

*She was quiet...*

Where did I learn all this in the first place, I wondered...

Love is incapable of hurting...
why did I cry and make people cry in the name of love...

*Instead of saying anything... the bird slowly moved and started slipping away...*

*Her smile was gone... and I slowly started smiling...*

Because I realised that if I love... I would never be hurt... and when I get hurt, I would not blame love for it...

My smile is precious, and I will watch out for the green bird now!

# Twenty Eight

## STORY OF THE SOUL

It is your story too... yet; it won't end when you
die...
it ends in every 'now'...

It is your story too... yet; it didn't start when you were
born...
it starts in every 'now'...

It is not a story, as you know stories...
it is just a collection of words... and a glimpse of the
canvas on which all stories unfold...
...

I can't find a beginning... and I can't see an end...
the beginning and the end are in time, and time lives
in me...
nothing moves in me with time, because time moves
in me...

I have travelled through ages...
I have lived each moment exactly how I am in this moment...

I am everything; yet, nothing is my real face...
I am the beauty, I am the beast...
I am the warrior, and I am the priest...

I was the one who locked the gas chambers, and I was the one who suffocated in them...
I was Romeo, I was Juliet and I was Shakespeare too...
I was the hand that held the sword, and I was the neck on which the sword fell...

I have seen everything...
and, all I have ever seen, is myself...

In this house of mirrors, I only see myself... all the time...

Still, my view is always fresh...
in each reflection, it is a different me...

All my reflections see me differently too...
I learn about me from all of them...

All I want from each reflection is to see me like never before...

So I go on creating as many different reflections as possible...

With great precision, I create imprecision; and with great order, I create chaos...

From a desire to make everyone equal, I make them all different...

Your soul is a reflection of mine too; your view of me is unique...

You have no parallel and you have no peer...
you are as much my reflection as a Buddha was...
and it is by careful design, that you are not like the Buddha...

If I needed to see through those eyes again, I would have created a million Buddhas by now...

I never repeat experiments, because my learning is permanent...
I learnt something when I created a saint, and I learnt something when I created a sinner...

Now I want to see from where you are...

No one can see like you, and no one can feel like you do...
no one has been where you are, and no one will ever be who you are...

Your unique view is your own personal soul...
you are valuable, because your view will never be there again...

Tomorrow, I will be seeing the world through new
eyes...
tomorrow, I will be making new mistakes...
tomorrow, when you won't be there I will be there...

But you will forever be part of my story... because you
are me...

Mine and yours is not a separate story...
you are just a wave in me... who is too busy watching
other waves...

When you say 'I', you walk away from me...
and when you say 'mine', you walk away from my reflection too...

You walk away collecting pebbles, and you call them
yours...

You walk away counting shadows, and call them yours...

Nothing is yours... but it all, might be you...

Like a wave contains the essence of the whole ocean,
each soul contains me completely...
like a bowl of water reflects the whole moon, I reflect
in my totality, in each of my reflection...

You ask me 'what will happen after my death?'...
I ask you where the moon goes, when you spill water...
you ask me 'what about my previous birth?'...

I ask you where the moon was, before the bowl was full...

If you want to understand this story, then don't question if there is life after death...
question whether you can live uniquely, before you die...

Don't wonder where your soul came from and where will it go...

Wonder how near you are to your soul...

The reading ends here... The Story, is being written!

# Twenty Nine

## ADVENTURE

*L* evel 1 - Just wait, just watch, just engage, just smile, just cry.

Level 2 - Villains appear, because the hero appears. Hero starts fighting for each toy and each space that is his.

Level 3 - Now he fights for each person that is his, and each dollar, which is his.

Level 4 – He learns to replace that which is lost, with similar things; replaces his partner with a new one, replaces his sword, his suit. He remains at this level until a dream catches his fancy.

Level 5 – He now wants to become the best he can be. He replaces beliefs, paths and methods few times. He enjoys fame and success, and, suffers failures. Finally, he sees the repetitive nature of challenges, and, notices the ticking of the clock for the first time. He gets worried, and questions his efforts.

Level 6 – Realisation. The game doesn't seem to be going anywhere. The same villains keep appearing over and over again. They have been there pretty much since level-2. Something needs to be done, before the timer ends.

Level 7 – Search. The scene is still as of an earlier level. But, the hero no longer fits in the scene. Although he faces the same challenges he faced earlier, it is a more difficult game now. That is because, now, he is trying to solve a different problem - the problem of transforming the character itself.

Level 8 - He is told that level-7 is solved. Life suddenly seems better, but, soon, he finds out that he is still stuck at an earlier level. This trick is played on him several times. He then questions the designer of game, and wonders out aloud, how is it that I am still stuck in the game when I have solved it...? Silence... No communication seems to reach the designer... Frustration, agony...

Level 9 - He realizes that it is by design that the designer does not respond... The game is not flawed and there is no fraud... He is exhausted... He surrenders...

Level 10 - Suddenly a door is seen where there was none all this while... He crosses the door and arrives exactly where he was... The door disappears...

Adventure continues, but, ends for him!

# *Thirty*

## TEACHER AND DISCIPLE

*Y*ou haven't heard any news of your love for a long
    time...
and a teacher comes and tells you, have faith, the one
you die for, is dying to see you too...

No wonder, you feel intoxicated with love...

You are stuck in this town filled with strangers...
no one understands you here...
you don't get to hear about your home often...
and he says he comes from your town...

No wonder, you ask so many questions...

You have been travelling for ages...
you get tired, you keep falling short of breath... you feel
like giving up...
and he says he comes back from the destination...

No wonder, he gives you hope...

You haven't seen your face for a while...
you have been too busy looking at others...
and he comes as a mirror... he makes you face yourself...

No wonder, you get confused and worried...

You have become cold... you have kept your doors closed for a long time...
you have not lit a candle in your place for a while... and he comes as a flame...

No wonder your eyes brighten up...
...

A teacher cannot give you your loved one...
it is just that near him, you get the fragrance of your love...

He cannot give you a map or travel for you... he just makes your journey feel worthwhile...

He didn't create the flame... the flame is because a fire touched him once...
...

It is for you to become a disciple to get something of value, from the teacher...
and, it is for the teacher to remain a student, to be able to give something of value, to you...

It is tough, but it is easy...
it is beyond reason, but, reasonably good...
a teacher and the disciple... it is an ultimate mismatch...
and yet, the perfect match...

Connected by their undying love for the same 'one', they walk together, as friends, but only one of them walks!

# *Thirty One*

## HOUSEWARMING

*N*o matter how much you paid... or will pay... you will always owe something to the house...

No matter what the contract says, you will always remain a debtor to your house...

The gift a house gives is ongoing, and, so should be your thankfulness...
it gives you the gift of freedom... freedom from the concerns of a basic need...
it sets you free, so you can focus on your love...

House is not something you own...
it is a place which you are fortunate to be in, every today...

House did not become yours just because you made a lot of money...

house became yours because it also wanted to be yours...
this space is as alive as you are...

House did not become yours because you made a good deal...
house is yours because this was the plan... not your plan though...

It comes as a gift of the divine... treat it with respect...
treat is as a living thing... do not burden it with clutter...
do not disrespect it in your frustrations with yourself...
do not neglect it and forget about it... just because it is always there for you...

And, keep evaluating your house often...
just so you know how much you have made on this house...

When you evaluate your house, keep these measures in your mind:

Value of a house is not measured in dollars...
it is measured by the number of stories you shared here... and by how much you each grew up, living in it...

Area of a house is not measured in square feet...
it is measured in disappearing distances, between its dwellers...

Nourishing power of a house is not measured by the cleanliness of air in it...

it is measured in portions... the portions of meals which are cooked in this house with a loving heart...
and which are shared with a smile...

Good fortune of a house is not defined by the north or east facing design...
it is measured by the good wishes left by the visitors...
by the number of people who entered the house and were welcomed whole-heartedly...

Utility of a house is not measured by the number of bedrooms or garages or balconies...
it is measured by number of smiles... number of times each of you smiled in this house without a reason...
...

If you remember the right measures for your house...
your house will always measure up to you...
...

Without changing the blueprint of a house and without touching a brick...
you can add value to the house and make it a home...

The design of a home, doesn't live on a piece of paper or in structures...
it lives, forever, on the hearts of those who lived in it...

May this home remain new for you every day...
as you sleep in this home, may you sleep as if you are done with life...

and as you wake up in this home, wake up as if you have a life to live...

May the hearts never get cold here and may the house-warming never end!

# Thirty Two

## BUDDHA RECALLS

### Four Noble truths

You are in love with an illusion called you!

Life forces you to break the illusion!!

You keep forgetting, life keeps reminding!!!

If you keep winning a life is lost!!!!

### Noble Eight-fold path

If you can ensure that no wave of your mind, passes
without telling you something about you...
if you can remain a student of life, even when it hurts...
if you seek change and not explanations...
or, if you just want to learn to love...
then that is 'Right Intention' (*Samyak sankalpa*)

If you can see that the other is exactly the same as you...
if you can accept, that no matter what, the other knows better about him/herself...
if you can see-through a person's appearance and habits, and see your own image...
or if you can just be in love with what you see... then that is 'Right View' *(Samyak drishti)*

If you see that your biggest challenge is within you...
and, if you have learned to face that challenge...
and, if no other challenge is more interesting than the challenge within you...
and, you put your efforts to face the challenge within you...
then, that is 'Right Effort' *(Samyak vyayama)*

If you can remember in each moment of excitement, that this shall pass too...
if you can remember in each moment of pain, that this shall pass too...
if you can remember that what you keep doing, is not your doing...
or, if you can remember to remember...
then, that is 'Right Mindfulness' *(Samyak smriti)*

If your attention is completely devoted to the interactions the universe is having with you...
if you can bring back your attention to what is being said...
if you can remain interested in everything that life presents in this moment...

or, if you can just love, and can focus without frowning...
then, that is 'Right Concentration' *(Samyak samadhi)*

If what you speak is not all about you...
if what you speak is not only for your pleasure or gain...
if what you speak is about who you are with, and not who you are...
if you don't have to remember what you said...
then, that is 'Right Speech' *(Samyak vacha)*

If your actions are the end, and not the means...
if you know what you do is never a charity for others...
if you act to participate, and not to gain...
if you act because you are here, not because who you are...
then that is 'Right Action' *(Samyak karmanta)*

If you do not own, what you earn...
if you are grateful for what you get...
if you completely agree with what you do...
if what you do, gives you shelter and bread...
then, whatever you do is 'Right Livelihood' *(Samyak ajiva)*

# Thirty Three

## PAIN OF DEATH

*S*he has been alone for ages...
she doesn't understand why you don't like her...
she has been looking for answers, since the beginning
of time...

She has been working faithfully to remove what no
longer belongs to the world of living...
she works continuously, and never stops helping your
world...

Yet, for some reason, you want her to remain hidden in
a lonely place...
you don't want to go there...
you have ensured that the place is as separated from
life, as it possibly can be...
what a lonely place for her to reside...

She feels happy when you light a candle in that place...

she is filled with joy for a moment, but candle soon burns out...
and, you always leave even before the candle starts to melt...

She is ugly, you say... but you say that without having ever looked at her face...
she is dark and evil, you say... but you say that, without ever meeting her...
...

She can see your love for her sister, called Birth...
when her sister arrives, there is always joy and celebration...

Death removes the perished piece by piece... so that Birth can create the new...
both of them work together all the time...

But, your discriminatory ways ensure that when Birth works, the work never goes unnoticed... and, when Death works, the work is ignored...

You ignore and hide her messages too...

She comes and reminds, you are getting old, and you hate her for that...
you focus on finding all sorts of tools to hide her messages...
promises of making her messages invisible keep coming...

You just don't want to see her footprints, you just don't want to hear her steps...
her footprints are in fallen leaves and in the wrinkles on your face; and, her steps sound like silence...
how much can you avoid?

What makes you love my sister so, so much and hate me so bitterly? she wonders...
when did you start seeing us as two, anyways...? my sister and I were never two...
...

She knows that you alone can answer these questions...

And, this is what she wrote to you today:

I have always loved you... and in my love, I send you messages...
my messages are to remind you to take care of each passing moment...
and if you ever think of me, think of my love for you...

You and I have come a long way together and we have not given up...
I haven't, because of my love for you, and you haven't, because you couldn't...

When you see my messages, see them as my reminders to you that you are precious...
you are precious, not because you will remain forever, but because you are so, so rare...

149

Our meeting will be precious too, you know... because we get to meet face to face only once...

When we meet, I will come with open arms...
I will bring bags full of your memories...

Your cherished moments, and your long forgotten ugly faces...

I will come prepared...

I will be so covered with things for you, that you will feel that you are meeting yourself...
for the very first time...

Will **you** be prepared for that meeting...

Will you appreciate me one day, and will you meet me with open arms, my love...

Yours,
Till dying do us part

# *Thirty Four*

## SMART, INTELLIGENT, BRILLIANT, GENIUS AND SIMPLE

I am Smart,
I have learned a few tricks... I know how to deal with people...
I am good at manipulating information to know what is best for me...
I feel good when I can cheat the system...
I want to be Intelligent though...

I am Intelligent,
I have mastered formulas, charts and graphs... I have mastered the rules of society...
I meticulously manipulate all my knowledge, to use it however it suits me...
I outplay Smart, and feel so good about it...
I want to be Brilliant someday...

I am Brilliant,

I have a unique way of manipulating information in each situation...

I can come up with ideas which Intelligent never thought of before...

I feel frustrated when I have to live with Smart and Intelligent...

I feel amazed by Genius though... I know I can never be like him...

I am Genius,

I have grown so much beyond Brilliant...

I am able to grasp information by just looking at it once...

I can come up with Brilliant's ideas, without too much churning of information in my head...

sometimes, I even connect to a place, where I can see the world in a new light...

from that place, I create ideas that change the world - ideas that Brilliant, then uses to feel more Brilliant...

I feel sorry for Smart, Intelligent and Brilliant... they have to work hard for what comes easy to me...

I am Simple,

In me lie the Smart, the Intelligent, the Brilliant and the Genius...

I know each particle in the universe is as smart as me... every cell in my body is more intelligent than me... each drop of water is more brilliant than me... and, each dry leaf is a work of genius...

I don't go through charts and graphs to know what is good for me...
I don't suffer through arguments and justifications to prove what is right...

I am like a blade of grass...
which just knows what to do next...

Like a river knows how to flow...
and, a tree knows how to grow...

I just know, how to know!

# Thirty Five

## SEEKING FREEDOM

What freedom do you seek?
freedom from the rules...
freedom from your work...
freedom from people in your life...

Think again, and be careful when you seek freedom...
don't become the fish that wanted to become free from
the sea...
one day, she succeeded; and she died...

The sea imposes restrictions on you...
may be these restrictions are to save your own life...
you need to be in the water... to live...

Your environment and the people in your life are things
that make you who you are...
you are in the sea, and the sea is in you... you can't be
free from anything, by going to a place far away...

there is no such place... seeking freedom from your here and now, is seeking the wrong freedom...

Seek the right freedom...
what makes you a slave, is your neediness...
seek freedom from your bondage and not your life...

Seek freedom from your desires and expectations, which make you a perpetual beggar...
you beg for love and attention in your relationships...
and, you beg for riches and recognitions in the world...
your bowl is different and your clothes are rich...
but, when you look at the shadow you make... you will, see a beggar...

Seek freedom, not from your conditions, but from your own conditioning...
do not run away, but run towards, those who show you your shadow...

Your chains don't disappear in a far-away place...
your chains don't disappear when you find someone new...
they remain intact, as long as you remain unchanged...
look within, and find all the chains which bind you...

Your chains are not in your activities... they are in who you are...

You want freedom to be able to choose more...

but it is your desire to exercise choice, that kills your freedom...

The moment you feel free... you run towards a new dream to tie you down...
of course, you don't want to be chained again...
but, you just fail to see that new pleasures you seek, will bring new chains too...

When you begin, the dream looks good...
but, you are yet to see, how it will feel when this dream comes true...
soon, the chains and hooks will appear, and it will be bondage again...
a fish never asks for the hook, it just can't help going for the bait...

Before you see another dream of freedom... have a look around...
maybe, you are living a dream right now...
a dream which you saw, a long time ago... and which came true, a long time ago...
maybe, you **are** free...

The moment you pick a path, all other paths become unavailable...
and there is always, just one path, on which you can be...
freedom is not in the path you are dreaming about...
freedom is to be free, on the path which you are on today...

You don't have to leave your path to be free...
you just have to realize, that when the time comes, then leaving this path will be as easy as finding it was...

You don't have to leave your comforts...
you just have to be the one who will laugh equally loud when these comforts are gone...

You don't have to leave the world...
you just have to ensure that you are not defined by the world...

And then, freedom will be found, in the most disciplined of circumstances...

Live free... or die trying!